CAPTAIN'S LOG—

Stardate: Earth, present day

Mission: To seek out the answers to 1001 questions about the cast, the writers, the episodes, the aliens, the planets, and the equipment that are all part of the fantastic *Star Trek* universe.

Orders: Take the 100 tantalizing quizzes created to test your *Star Trek* trivia knowledge, and have fun doing it!

That Is All ... Mission Accomplished ... Over And Out ...

SIGNET Books for the Trivia Fan

☐ **THE OFFICIAL TV TRIVIA QUIZ BOOK by Bart Andrews.** (#Y6363—$1.25)

☐ **THE OFFICIAL TV TRIVIA QUIZ BOOK #2 by Bart Andrews.** (#Y7187—$1.25)

☐ **THE OFFICIAL ROCK AND ROLL TRIVIA QUIZ BOOK by Marc Sotkin.** (#Y7407—$1.25)

☐ **THE NOSTALGIA QUIZ BOOK by Martin A. Gross.** (#W7384—$1.50)

☐ **THE NOSTALGIA QUIZ BOOK #2 by Martin A. Gross.** (#Y6554—$1.25)

☐ **THE NOSTALGIA QUIZ BOOK #3 by Martin A. Gross.** (#Y7226—$1.25)

☐ **THE SPORTS NOSTALGIA QUIZ BOOK by Zander Hollander and David Schulz.** (#Y6318—$1.25)

☐ **THE SPORTS NOSTALGIA QUIZ BOOK #2 by Zander Hollander and David Schulz.** (#Y7365—$1.25)

The
Star Trek
Quiz Book

*1,001 Trivia
Teasers for Trekkies*

by Bart Andrews
with
Brad Dunning

A SIGNET BOOK
NEW AMERICAN LIBRARY
TIMES MIRROR

NAL BOOKS ARE ALSO AVAILABLE AT DISCOUNTS
IN BULK QUANTITY FOR INDUSTRIAL OR
SALES-PROMOTIONAL USE. FOR DETAILS, WRITE TO
PREMIUM MARKETING DIVISION, NEW AMERICAN LIBRARY, INC.,
1301 AVENUE OF THE AMERICAS, NEW YORK, NEW YORK 10019.

Ⓞ

SIGNET, SIGNET CLASSICS, MENTOR, PLUME AND MERIDIAN BOOKS
are published by The New American Library, Inc.,
1310 Avenue of the Americas, New York, New York 10019

FIRST SIGNET PRINTING, JUNE, 1977

1 2 3 4 5 6 7 8 9

PRINTED IN THE UNITED STATES OF AMERICA

For
my sister CATHY
who, like *Star Trek*,
is out of this world!

RANDOM NOTES

It's September, 1966. The National Broadcasting Company unleashes its seasonal cache of new TV shows, ballyhooing them as "the greatest premiere attractions in television history." Great attractions like *Hey, Landlord*, *The Roger Miller Show*, *The Monkees*, *The Road West*, *Occasional Wife*, *The Girl from U.N.C.L.E.*, *Tarzan*, *The Hero*, *T.H.E. Cat*, and—of course—*Star Trek*.

The peacock-symbol network gives the hour-long science fiction series its Thursday-at-8:30 P.M. slot, tenuously sandwiched between *Daniel Boone* (in its third season) and *The Hero* (a new sitcom from the producers of *Get Smart!* that will fade by midseason), and up against CBS's formidable *My Three Sons* (in its seventh, motherless season) and the *Thursday Night Movie*, and ABC's *Tammy Grimes Show* (one of TV's biggest disasters) and *Bewitched* (one of TV's biggest hits).

Despite these programming difficulties, *Star Trek* somehow found its audience—an unbelievably loyal bunch—and remained on the air three seasons, making it NBC's longest-running, new (1966) series. Its ratings were never spectacular. In fact, the show was on the verge of cancellation after its second year. Five hundred Caltech students showed up at NBC's Burbank headquarters and led a vociferous protest march; and every science fiction magazine in existence launched wide-reaching campaigns to stop the cancellation. Canadian fans in British Columbia even took out and paid for newspaper ads proclaiming, "Unite to Save the Show." In a week's time, 16,000 letters of protest had arrived at NBC executive offices, and by the end of three months, one million expressions of disappointment— not to mention outright horror—had been tallied by network statisticians. The result, of course, was that *Star Trek* was saved, for another year.

The show ended its network run on June 3, 1969, with the telecast of "Turnabout Intruder." But eight years or so later, the seventy-eight existing color episodes are still running in syndication in over 150 domestic TV markets and in a large number of foreign countries, a tribute to *Star Trek*'s loyal followers. This faithful cult of fans, who have become known as Trekkies (they don't like the label), became the major force in keeping the show—and its boundless spirit—alive.

To term the "movement" a mere phenomenon would be an injustice. When the first "official" *Star Trek* convention took place in 1972 at New York's Commodore Hotel, a handful of fans was expected to attend. What happened? Thirty-five hundred card-carrying Trekkies showed up and there was bedlam. A year later, 7,000 people showed up, each paying five bucks admission, and more had to be turned away at the door. They came from all over the world to mingle with their peers and exchange such dubious curiosities as "authentic" Vulcan pendants and pointed ears made of Latex.

In assembling the material for this book, I was fortunate enough to have the help of some of these staunch fans— Debby Anderson, George Switzer, and James F. Engelhardt—and three more *Star Trek* devotees who deserve *much* more than a casual thank you—Joanne Bennett, Jane Kaplan, and, of course, Constance Colman.

An extra special acknowledgment must be made to my assistant, Brad Dunning, who did a magnificent job . . . as usual.

BART ANDREWS

Hollywood, California

QUESTIONS

1. TREK TEASERS

1. Can you recall the exact premiere date?

2. Which network carried the series?

3. What connection did Lucille Ball have with *Star Trek?*

4. Of the eight principal characters, which one did not appear during the first season?

5. Where were the main components of the *Enterprise* assembled?

6. Where was Dr. McCoy born?

7. Who played Spock's parents?

8. What common twentieth-century kitchen utensils were used on the show as super-sophisticated medical instruments?

9. Where is most of the *Enterprise*'s engine circuitry located?

10. Where did Uhura get her name?

2. WHO SAID THAT?

Which Enterprise *officer said the following, and in what episode?*

1. "Tell me how your planet looks on a lazy spring night when the moon is full."

2. "You were about to make a medical comment?"

3. "Well, Mr. Spock, letting yourself be hit on the head is not a method King Solomon would have approved."

4. "Well, what do you know—I finally got the last word."

5. "Take it easy, lad. Everybody's entitled to an opinion."

6. "Let's get the hell out of here."

7. "We all have to take a chance, especially if one is all you have."

8. "Don't ever tell him I said he was the best First Officer in the fleet."

9. "In a pig's eye!"

10. "I don't know what you're so mad about. It isn't every First Officer who gets to belt his Captain ... several times."

3. CAPTAIN'S LOG

Can you identify the episode from the opening stardate?

1. 4523.3
2. 1513.1
3. 4598.0
4. 3842.3
5. 3219.4
6. 4513.3
7. 5423.4
8. 4385.3
9. 3372.7
10. 5928.5

4. SPACE NOSTALGIA

1. What color are the science officers' uniforms?

2. Name Uhura's mother.

3. In which three episodes did Uhura sing?

4. Whom did McCoy replace as the Senior Surgeon aboard the *Enterprise?*

5. In which two episodes was ex-*Enterprise* Captain Christopher Pike mentioned?

6. Half-speed is what warp factor?

7. Kirk logged the stardates in the improper sequential order in what episode?

8. In the episode "Arena," to whom did Spock refer as being "an experienced combat officer"?

9. Who told Spock he was "ill-mannered"?

10. What is the darkest planet Kirk has ever seen?

5. ROLE CALL

Match the people behind-the-scenes with their position or responsibility.

1. Jim Rugg
2. Joe D'Agosta
3. Fred Philips
4. Bill Theiss
5. Marc Daniels
6. Jerry Finnerman
7. Charlie Washburn
8. Herb Solow
9. Bob Justman
10. D. C. Fontana

a. Special effects
b. Cinematographer
c. Producer
d. Makeup
e. Script Editor
f. Assistant Director
g. Costume Designer
h. Director
i. Casting
j. Vice-President of Desilu, Inc.

/5

6. VOYAGES

Can you identify the episode from these clues?

1. Mr. Spock pretends to be a Vulcan trader on the planet Organia.

2. Captain Kirk almost becomes a victim of a neural neutralizer.

3. The crew of the *Enterprise* takes a vacation on a most unusual planet, where their thoughts and fantasies instantly materialize.

4. Captain Kirk engages in a battle with an alien creature named Gorn.

5. For a short time, Professor Crater's wife, Nancy, is the same as McCoy remembers her.

6. Commodore Matt Decker attempts to destroy a huge alien weapon by driving a shuttlecraft into its center.

7. Dr. McCoy thinks he has only a year to live when he permits the Instrument of Obedience to be implanted.

8. McCoy and Spock activate Kirk's post-death visual tape.

9. Captain Kirk disappears into a mysterious obelisk.

10. Spock is wounded on planet Neural.

7. CARTOON TREK

The following queries pertain to the animated version of Star Trek.

1. In "The Ambergris Element," what is the method which turns air-breathers into water-breathers?

2. What is the name of the *Enterprise* shuttlecraft used in "Slaver Weapon"?

3. On what planet is Dr. McCoy arrested for mass murder in "Albatross"?

4. In "Practical Joker," what does Scotty receive from a food machine instead of the sandwich he orders?

5. On what planet would you find a Swooper?

6. In "One of Our Planets Is Missing," what part of the cosmic cloud does Scotty use to regenerate the *Enterprise*'s engines?

7. In "Lorelei Signal," what female crew member takes control of the *Enterprise*?

8. Lucien refers to Spock as his "elfin friend" in what animated segment?

9. What is the name of the Klingon battle cruiser in "More Tribbles, More Troubles"?

10. In which episode are people encountered who are born old?

8. CAPTAIN JAMES T. KIRK

1. In what state was Kirk born?

2. Name Kirk's deceased brother.

3. Recall the Captain's serial number.

4. Who piloted the *Enterprise* before Kirk?

5. On what deck is the Captain's quarters?

6. Which American President does Kirk idolize?

7. How old was Kirk when he entered the Space Academy?

8. What female scientist did Jim once consider marrying?

9. In what episode was Kirk forced to slap himself?

10. As a midshipman at the Space Academy, with whom did Kirk fall in love?

9. CAST OF CHARACTERS

Can you name the episode in which these characters appeared?

1. Captain Ramart, Tom Nellis, Thasian, Tina Lawton
2. Tellarite, Garth of Izar, Marta, Donald Cory
3. Steve O'Connel, Don Linden, Ray Tsingtao, Gorgan
4. Sirah, Wu, Cloud William, Dr. Carter
5. Morla, Kara, Sybo, Tark
6. Ruk, Andrea, Rayburn, Dr. Brown
7. Gem, Lal, Thann, Dr. Linke
8. Tongo Rad, Adam, Mavig, Irini Galliulin
9. Midro, Plasus, Vanna, Anka
10. Admiral Fitzgerald, Hodin, Krodak, Odona

10. VULCANS NEVER BLUFF

Name the Star Trek *segment in which Mr. Spock said the following.*

1. "I'd advise ya to keep dialing."

2. "He knows, Doctor. He has reasoned it out."

3. "I found it an accelerating experience."

4. "No one can guarantee the actions of another."

5. "I'm sure the Captain would simply have said, 'Forget it, Bones.'"

6. "The most unfortunate lack in current computer programming is that there is nothing available to immediately replace the starship surgeon."

7. "Commander, your attire is not only more important, it should actually stimulate our conversation."

8. "I had no idea they were trained, Doctor. From watching you I assumed it was trial and error."

9. "I am a Vulcan. I am a Vulcan. There is no pain."

10. "Sir, there is a multi-legged creature crawling on your shoulder."

11. WRITER'S CAMP

Match the episode with its writer.

1. "The Man Trap"   a. Gene Roddenberry
2. "The Menagerie"   b. Lee Cronin
3. "The Devil in the
   Dark"   c. George C. Johnson
4. "The City on the Edge
   of Forever"   d. Harlan Ellison
5. "The Doomsday Ma-
   chine"   e. Gene L. Coon
6. "Spectre of the Gun"   f. Lee Erwin
7. "Friday's Child"   g. David Gerrold
8. "The Trouble with
   Tribbles"   h. D. C. Fontana
9. "Turnabout Intruder"   i. Arthur H. Singer
10. "Whom Gods Destroy"   j. Norman Spinrad

12. THE U.S.S. *ENTERPRISE*

1. On what deck is the medical lab located?

2. Name the three principal operational divisions to which crew members are assigned.

3. What is the maximum number of people or objects that can be beamed to or from the main operational transporter?

4. How many translucent viewing screens are on the bridge?

5. What is the name of the shuttlecraft stored inside the *Enterprise*?

6. In all but one episode, the *Enterprise* is shown moving left to right. Which episode showed the Starship moving right to left?

7. For how many years can the *Enterprise* be self-sustaining in space?

8. Who created plans and designs for the *Enterprise*?

9. Within fifty feet, how long is the U.S.S. *Enterprise*?

10. How many crew members aboard?

13. MR. SPOCK

1. Which of Spock's parents was Vulcan?

2. What is Spock's bridge position?

3. Why are his ears pointed?

4. What color is Spock's blood?

5. How long has he served on the *Enterprise*?

6. What is the typical Vulcan life span?

7. What was Spock's mother's occupation?

8. Where is his heart located?

9. What did Spock's father wish his son to become?

10. Besides Spock, how many other Vulcans serve on board the *Enterprise*?

14. PLANET PUZZLE

Match the episode with the planet on which the action takes place.

1. Ardana

2. Holberg 917G

3. Pyris VII

4. Organia

5. Pollux IV

6. Eminiar VII

7. Exo III

8. Beta III

9. Janus VI

10. Capella IV

a. "Errand for Mercy"

b. "Friday's Child"

c. "The Cloud Miners"

d. "What Are Little Girls Made Of?"

e. "The Return of the Archons"

f. "A Taste of Armageddon"

g. "Requiem for Methuselah"

h. "The Devil in the Dark"

i. "Catspaw"

j. "Who Mourns for Adonais?"

15. ON THE AIR

1. Who created "tribbles"?

2. What was the title of Gene Roddenberry's original pilot script?

3. What was the last episode of *Star Trek* titled?

4. According to the opening narration, how long was the *Enterprise*'s mission to last?

5. In what century was the series set?

6. What musical instrument did Spock play?

7. What is the Klingon version of the phaser called?

8. Name Dr. McCoy's daughter.

9. How many seats inside the shuttlecraft *Galileo*?

10. Where is the Spock "pinch" applied?

16. TEST PATTERNS

1. What is a tricorder?

2. In what episode did Gene Roddenberry's daughter Dawn appear?

3. What color is the sky on Planet Vulcan?

4. Roddenberry's pilot script was later transformed into what award-winning two-part episode?

5. Who is third in command aboard the *Enterprise*?

6. What is Chekov's first name?

7. Who referred to Spock as "Mr. Ears"?

8. Who, other than Kirk, sat facing the viewing screen on the bridge?

9. How many pockets do the uniforms of the *Enterprise* crew members have?

10. What are Class M worlds?

17. WITH SPECIAL GUEST STAR . . .

Match the guest star with the character he or she portrayed.

1. Lt. Cmdr. Gary
   Mitchell

   a. Ricardo Montalban

2. Miri

   b. Tige Andrews

3. Khan Singh

   c. Robert Lansing

4. Charlie Evans

   d. Lee Meriwether

5. Balok

   e. Gary Lockwood

6. Amanda

   f. William Windom

7. Commodore Matt
   Decker

   g. Kim Darby

8. Kras

   h. Clint Howard

9. Gary Seven

   i. Robert Walker, Jr.

10. Losira

    j. Jane Wyatt

18. TRIPLE THREAT

Recall who said the following and to whom they were speaking, and name the episode.

1. "The fat's on the fire now."

2. "Why don't you go chase an asteroid?"

3. "You sing and dance as well as anyone I've ever seen."

4. "I call them ears."

5. "You're an idealistic dreamer."

6. "Perhaps they made me out of dreams you've forgotten."

7. "War has its fortune—good and bad."

8. "Chess? Billiards? Conversation?"

9. "That's a girl."

10. "Look at those pine trees."

19. FIRST AND FOREMOST

1. Name the premiere episode of *Star Trek*.

2. Do you recall the first four words of the opening narration?

3. In which episode were the Klingons first featured?

4. In which segment was the Vulcan mind touch first observed?

5. Ensign Chekov first apppeared in what episode?

6. Who was the first crewman to have a tribble?

7. In what episode did Spock first call Kirk "Jim"?

8. What is Lt. Scott's first name?

9. In what episode was the Vulcan pendant first worn?

10. Which segment contained American television's first interracial kiss?

20. THE VERSATILES

Match the two characters who were played by the same person, and identify the actor or actress.

1. Melakon ("Patterns of Force")

2. Nomad ("The Changeling")

3. Dr. Anne Mulhall ("Return to Tomorrow")

4. Darnell ("The Man Trap")

5. Thasian ("Charlie X")

6. Joe Tormolen ("The Naked Time")

7. Dr. Simon van Gelder ("Dagger of the Mind")

8. Mirt ("A Piece of the Action")

9. Ensign Harper ("The Ultimate Computer")

10. Ensign Freeman ("The Trouble with Tribbles")

a. Black Knight ("Shore Leave")

b. Ensign Mallory ("The Apple")

c. Dr. Miranda Jones ("Is There In Truth No Beauty?")

d. Dr. Sevrin ("The Way to Eden")

e. Tharn ("Mirror, Mirror")

f. Lieutenant O'Neil ("The Tholian Web")

g. Captain Ronald Tracey ("The Omega Glory")

h. Ensign Jordan ("I, Mudd")

i. Melkot ("Spectre of the Gun")

j. Hanar ("By Any Other Name")

21. CHARACTER STUDY

From the brief information given, identify the character.

1. Used the name of Leo Walsh and added yet another criminal offense to an already lengthy, deviant record.

2. He is dispatched from the Omaha Air Base.

3. Kingpin of the Southside Territory.

4. A highly touted attorney, according to Areel Shaw.

5. Worships great leaders of the past.

6. Hung out at the 21st Street Mission to assist those less fortunate.

7. The woman with the deadly touch.

8. A bearer of furry nuisances.

9. Attempts a Henry Higgins-like undertaking, but fails dramatically.

10. She has a son named Peter.

11. Convinces McCoy to submit to an implantation of an Instrument of Obedience.

22. "THE MAN TRAP"

1. What is the purpose of the *Enterprise* mission on Planet M113?

2. What form did the creature take to lure Darnell?

3. What was the apparent cause of Darnell's death?

4. Do you recall Nancy's nickname for McCoy?

5. What identity does the creature take to gain entrance to the *Enterprise*?

6. Who or what is Beauregard?

7. What did Uhura tell Spock she'd do if the word "frequency" was used again?

8. What Space Commander was mentioned in reference to a "special order"?

9. Name the animal species on earth that Crater compared his creature to.

10. What chemical does the creature crave?

23. "CHARLIE X"

1. How old is Charlie?

2. On what planet was Charlie raised?

3. What vessel transfers Charlie to the *Enterprise* and is later destroyed?

4. How did Charlie's parents die?

5. Who is the first female Charlie sees?

6. How many moves do we see Spock make before he defeats Charlie in a chess match?

7. What did Charlie cause to appear in the ship's ovens instead of the meat loaf originally placed there?

8. Where does Charlie want the *Enterprise* to take him?

9. Whom does Charlie consider a father figure?

10. What did Charlie do to Tina Lawton after Yeoman Rand introduced them?

24. "WHERE NO MAN HAS GONE BEFORE"

1. Who destroyed the U.S.S. *Valiant*?

2. What was the transporter called in this episode?

3. What after-effect does Mitchell suffer from moments after the encounter?

4. To protect his ship, where does Kirk plan to leave Mitchell?

5. What is the relationship between Kirk and Mitchell?

6. How does Mitchell kill Lt. Kelso?

7. Who escapes with Mitchell on the planet?

8. With what weapon does Kirk hunt Mitchell?

9. How does Mitchell attempt to kill Kirk?

10. As Kirk is about to smash Mitchell's skull, what does he say?

25. "THE NAKED TIME"

1. Name the planet about to disintegrate.

2. Who was the first crewman to contract the virus and what trait did he reveal?

3. With what two graffiti proclamations did Dr. Harrison deface corridor walls?

4. How is the virus spread?

5. What effect does the virus have on Sulu?

6. What exactly does Spock do inside Briefing Room 2?

7. Where does Riley ensconce himself to sing, much to the dismay of other crew members, "I'll Take You Home Again, Kathleen"?

8. Who received Nurse Chapel's display of affections?

9. What were the odds against repairing the ship's engines before hitting the Psi 2000 atmosphere?

10. Where does Riley announce his formal dance will be held?

26. "THE ENEMY WITHIN"

1. Which crewman's clothing becomes contaminated, thus causing the transporter to malfunction?

2. Name the deck and room number of Yeoman Rand.

3. What piece of equipment did Scott send Technician Wilson for?

4. What mineral on the planet caused the contamination?

5. Whom did Kirk's "evil" half meet in the Transporter Room and beat unconscious?

6. How cold does Alfa 177 become at night?

7. How many crewmen are left on the planet because of the transporter malfunction?

8. What three qualities did Spock claim belonged to the "evil" Kirk?

9. What three qualities did Spock declare belonged to the "good" Kirk?

10. Name the part of the transporter that the "evil" Kirk destroyed with his phaser.

27. "MUDD'S WOMEN"

1. Do you recall the names of the three women?

2. What three crimes has Mudd been convicted of?

3. What was Mudd's punishment for the crimes?

4. Who called Mudd a jackass?

5. What was unusual about Ruth's home planet?

6. How many brothers did Eve have?

7. How many lithium crystals did the *Enterprise* need?

8. What was the name of the card game that Eve played on Rigel XII?

9. What color were the Venus drug pills?

10. Since Kirk is maritally unavailable, whom does Eve decide to pursue?

28. "WHAT ARE LITTLE GIRLS MADE OF?"

1. What is the surface temperature of Exo III?

2. How many previous expeditions did Kirk embark on to find Korby?

3. What was the name of Korby's assistant?

4. What career did Chapel forsake to join the *Enterprise*?

5. To what colony did George Samuel Kirk wish to be transferred?

6. Who created Ruk?

7. To whom does Chapel bestow the title of "mechanical geisha"?

8. Why did Korby create an android to replace his own body?

9. How is Matthews killed?

10. How was Korby able to revolutionize immunization techniques?

29. "MIRI"

1. What was the name of the project that scientists on Miri's planet were working on when the disease developed?

2. What was the aging rate for the children?

3. When do the children eventually contract the disease?

4. What is a "grup"?

5. McCoy wanted what two instruments beamed down from the *Enterprise?*

6. What three-hundred-year-old musical instrument did Miri have in her home?

7. How did the children refer to the communicators?

8. Who was the male leader of the children?

9. Why does Miri change her mind about helping the crew?

10. What do the children call themselves?

30. "DAGGER OF THE MIND"

1. What penal colony is being investigated?

2. On whose insistence does Kirk order an inquiry?

3. What was written on the side of the capsule in which Van Gelder hid?

4. How large a dose of sedative did it take to subdue Van Gelder?

5. What was the name of the transporter technician who tried to use the transporter while the colony's force field was in operation?

6. What device is Dr. Adams using to inhumanly drain patients' brains?

7. While demonstrating the device, what sensation does Noel first implant in Kirk's brain?

8. How does Dr. Noel finally reach the power controls of the colony?

9. Who learns, through Van Gelder, of the evil doings at the penal colony?

10. How is Dr. Adams killed?

31. "THE CORBOMITE MANEUVER"

1. Why is Kirk in Sick Bay?

2. What endocrine gland does Spock suugest be removed from Lt. Bailey?

3. Who referred to the cube as "flypaper"?

4. What food did Rand serve Kirk in his quarters?

5. Name the alien vessel.

6. What is Bailey's position?

7. How long did Bailey give the *Enterprise* to prepare for its destruction?

8. Whom did the first Balok remind Spock of?

9. What title does Bailey acquire when he joins Balok?

10. Name the libation consumed to seal friendly relations between the cultures.

32. "THE MENAGERIE" (PART ONE)

1. How did Captain Pike become disfigured?

2. What is the punishment for disobeying General Order 7?

3. Who is the Commander of Starbase 11?

4. What element was the outside of the shuttlecraft made of?

5. Whom did Spock put in operational command of the *Enterprise* when he surrendered himself for arrest?

6. How many planets in the Talos system?

7. Vina is the survivor of what starship?

8. Where was the *Enterprise* heading before answering the Talos IV signal?

9. What type of atomic rays injured Pike?

10. Who was a mutual friend of Kirk and Miss Piper?

33. "THE MENAGERIE" (PART TWO)

1. How many times did Spock admit his guilt?

2. Why did the Talosians release Pike and his *Enterprise* crew members?

3. Why did Vina choose to stay on Talos IV?

4. What was the name of Pike's horse that the Talosians recreated?

5. What type of explosion did the overload of Number One's phaser result in?

6. What weapon did Pike possess during his fights with the Kalar?

7. Why did the Talosians create the court-martial?

8. In one of Pike's illusions, Vina resembles a temptress from what planet?

9. Who freed the *Enterprise* crew when he saw they were going to be of no use to the Talosians?

10. From whom does Kirk get authorization to allow Pike to remain on Talos IV?

34. "THE CONSCIENCE OF THE KING"

1. On what planet were four thousand people put to death, and why?

2. What did Lenore call Kirk?

3. Name the Shakespearean play being performed in Arthurian dress.

4. What song does Lt. Uhura sing?

5. What poison was given to Lt. Riley?

6. Name the ship that was supposed to transport the Karidian players to Benecia.

7. Do you recall the romantic, though prejudicial, words Captain Kirk recited to Lenore?

8. How does Kodos die?

9. What effect does his death have on Lenore?

10. Under what diocese are the Karidian Players?

35. "BALANCE OF TERROR"

1. What was Kirk doing when Outpost 4 was attacked?

2. What is the purpose of Outpost 4?

3. Who is the head of the Romulan Empire?

4. According to Spock's charts, what is the name of one of the suns in the Romulan system?

5. Name the Commander of Outpost 4.

6. Why didn't the Romulans know the *Enterprise* was in pursuit?

7. What was the name of the comet that the Romulans penetrated in hopes of eluding the *Enterprise*?

8. What Romulan was reduced two ranks for sending a message and breaking silence?

9. Who was the only person killed aboard the *Enterprise*?

10. What made Stiles change his mind about Vulcans?

36. "SHORE LEAVE"

1. In what region was the shore leave planet?

2. Who becomes Dr. McCoy's companion?

3. What section of the *Enterprise* was first to beam down for R and R (rest and relaxation)?

4. Who "kills" McCoy?

5. Name Kirk's old girlfriend who appears, detaining the Captain on the surface.

6. From what planet are McCoy's cabaret girls?

7. Whom did Yeoman Barrows dream about only to find the dream come true?

8. Who is older—Finnegan or Kirk?

9. Whom does Sulu cause to materialize?

10. What kind of plane attacks Lt. Rodriguez and Angela?

37. "THE *GALILEO* SEVEN"

1. Name the Federation official onboard to supervise the transfer of the medical supplies.

2. What is the *Galileo* sent out to investigate?

3. Which two crewmen of the *Galileo* were killed?

4. What planet did the *Galileo* crash on?

5. Who thought a proper burial for the dead *Galileo* crewmen took precedence over the surviving passengers' escape?

6. To what important American archeological find of 1925 did Spock refer?

7. How many pounds did the *Galileo* have to shed before a lift-off could safely occur?

8. Which colony needs the medical supplies?

9. How much time was left after Spock jettisoned the fuel pods?

10. Why did Spock release the fuel?

38. "THE SQUIRE OF GOTHOS"

1. Who was the navigator in this episode?

2. According to Trelane, who had "the face that launched a thousand ships"?

3. What is an empty area of space called?

4. Name the three charges brought against Kirk in Trelane's court.

5. How many medals adorned Trelane's uniform?

6. Name the meteorologist who accompanied the landing party.

7. Who does Trelane say is "as beautiful as the Queen of Sheba"?

8. Where was the *Enterprise* headed before Trelane's diversion?

9. How is Kirk saved from death by Trelane?

10. What words does Trelane repeat seven times as he fades away?

39. "ARENA"

1. Who invites the *Enterprise* crewmen to Cestus III?

2. Name the crewman who was killed by the Gorns.

3. What was the rank of the only living Cestus III survivor?

4. Who was the *Enterprise* navigator in this episode?

5. What human instinct does Kirk feel toward the Gorn?

6. What valuable crystalline mineral is found in abundance on the asteroid?

7. For what does Kirk proclaim he would trade all the minerals on the asteroid?

8. What does the Captain combine to make gunpowder?

9. What type of weapon does Kirk create to wound the Gorn?

10. What is the Metron wearing when he appears before Kirk?

40. "TOMORROW IS YESTERDAY"

1. What were the code names of Captain Christopher's plane and home base?

2. Christopher and Spock both doubted the existence of what?

3. What decade is it on earth when the *Enterprise* arrives?

4. Where was the ship's computer recently repaired?

5. What was the result of the overhaul?

6. Who questions Kirk at Omaha Air Base?

7. What method did the *Enterprise* use to return to the twenty-second century?

8. What was Christopher's son to be named, and what important role would he play in history?

9. What food did the air police sergeant request while aboard the *Enterprise*?

10. To what agency did Kirk tell Captain Christopher the *Enterprise* was under authority?

41. "COURT-MARTIAL"

1. What were the charges against Kirk?

2. On what Starbase does the trial take place?

3. What other orbiting starship was mentioned?

4. How long had it been since Kirk had seen Areel Shaw?

5. What lawyer did Areel recommend?

6. How many times does Spock defeat the computer in chess matches?

7. In Cogley's opinion, what is far superior to computers?

8. What was Finney's daughter's first name?

9. Name the friend who shuns Kirk on Starbase 11.

10. What was the name of the starship on which Finney and Kirk served?

42. "THE RETURN OF THE ARCHONS"

1. Who is the first *Enterprise* crewman to be absorbed by Landru?

2. How many years ago did the *Archon* disappear?

3. What was the name of Reger's daughter?

4. Name the event that is a means for members of the Body to release pent-up aggression.

5. Who saves Kirk and Spock from the Body?

6. What is the Red Hour?

7. Who attacks Tula during the festival?

8. Who stays on Beta III to begin rehabilitating the society?

9. How long has the scientist who programmed the computer been dead?

10. When the landing party first arrives, where are they thought to be from?

43. "SPACE SEED"

1. What ancient ship of the obsolete DY-100 class does the *Enterprise* encounter?

2. By what means are the crewmen of the spaceship kept alive?

3. They are the survivors of what twentieth-century war?

4. Who is the leader of these survivors?

5. What does the leader wish to read while recuperating in Sick Bay?

6. Where does Khan place Kirk to torture him in hopes of "persuading" the other members of the *Enterprise* to join his ranks?

7. Who finally comes to Kirk's rescue?

8. According to Khan, what did he have to offer the twentieth-century world?

9. Where are Khan and his followers to be exiled?

10. What two punishment alternatives does Lt. McGivers have?

44. "A TASTE OF ARMAGEDDON"

1. Who has been sent by the Federation to set up diplomatic relations with Eminiar VII?

2. Who greets the landing party on the planet?

3. How long have Eminiar VII and Vendikar been at war?

4. What controls the entire war and its victims?

5. Who is the First Councilman of the Eminian Union?

6. How long does Kirk tell Scotty to wait before enacting General Order 24?

7. What two disintegration chambers are destroyed?

8. Kirk has his own name for these disintegration areas. Do you recall it?

9. Who does Anan 7 call a barbarian?

10. What Federation starship was destroyed fifty years before the *Enterprise* arrived at Eminiar VII?

45. "THIS SIDE OF PARADISE"

1. What type of rays are constantly showering on Omicron Ceti III?

2. How long will humans live after exposure to the rays?

3. What is Leila's occupation?

4. Who is the leader of the colonists?

5. How long have Spock and Leila known each other?

6. How does Kirk break the effect the spores have on Spock?

7. What has Spock seen on Berengaria VII?

8. What triggers Kirk's emotions, breaking the grip of the spores' effect?

9. Which Starbase is nearby?

10. How does Kirk free his crew and colonists?

46. "THE DEVIL IN THE DARK"

1. What is the main purpose for the colony on Janus VI?

2. At what level is contact made with the monster?

3. How did the creature kill miners?

4. What is the monster called?

5. Who communicated the distress signal to the *Enterprise*?

6. What does Spock think of Kirk's decision to destroy the monster?

7. Who is in charge of security on the planet?

8. What words does the monster burn into a nearby rock after being wounded?

9. What did McCoy use to repair the monster's wound?

10. What humanoid feature did the monster find most attractive?

47. "ERRAND OF MERCY"

1. How does Organia rate on the culture scale?

2. Who greets Spock and Kirk on the planet?

3. When the Klingons arrive, how does Spock disguise himself?

4. What does Kirk say his name is?

5. Even though Kirk is outfitted as an Organian, what does Kor notice as being different from a typical Organian?

6. What does Kor promise the Organians if a single Klingon soldier is killed?

7. What is Kirk's answer to Kor's request, "Tell me about the dispersal of Starfleet"?

8. Which Organian council member possesses clairvoyant powers?

9. How does the Organian council prevent violence?

10. According to the Organians, what unbelievable quality will the Klingons acquire in the future?

48. "THE ALTERNATIVE FACTOR"

1. To which high-ranking official did Kirk speak when he received the message from Star Fleet Command?

2. How many dilithium crystals did Lazarus A and B take from the *Enterprise*?

3. Whom does Lazarus A render unconscious in order to steal his dilithium crystals?

4. Name the section of Lazarus's ship that enabled him to enter the alternative warp.

5. Of what substance was Lazarus's planet composed?

6. Why does Lazarus want the dilithium crystals?

7. What was Lazarus's body temperature?

8. What would happen if Lazarus A and Lazarus B were to meet in the same universe?

9. Which Lazarus is irrational and potentially dangerous?

10. What was Lazarus doing when his planet was being destroyed?

49. "THE CITY ON THE EDGE OF FOREVER"

1. What drug causes McCoy to become a time traveler?

2. Name the two boxers appearing at Madison Square Garden, according to the poster seen when Spock and Kirk first beam to New York.

3. Name the social worker to whom Kirk becomes attached.

4. What is the room number of Kirk and Spock's apartment?

5. What wages were offered to Kirk and Spock for ten hours of work?

6. At what theater was the Clark Gable movie playing?

7. What three words does Kirk tell Edith replace "I love you"?

8. "FDR Confers With Slum Angel" was the headline of what newspaper?

9. If Edith is saved by McCoy, how will that ultimately cause the downfall of the United States?

10. What song was playing on the radio when Kirk and Edith were walking home?

50. "OPERATION—ANNIHILATE!"

1. What planet is suffering from an epidemic of mass insanity?

2. What was Jim Kirk's brother's name and occupation?

3. Which one of the *Enterprise* officers had visited Deneva before and in what capacity?

4. How many Denevans were in the group that attacked the landing party?

5. How long ago, according to Kirk's sister-in-law, Aurelan, had the creatures arrived?

6. What were Aurelan Kirk's last words before she died?

7. On what part of the human body does the mysterious creature attach itself?

8. The flying creatures are found to be only a single cell from what part of a whole creature?

9. What does Captain Kirk consider the most difficult decision of his life?

10. Mr. Spock bravely turned human guinea pig to test a theory of Dr. McCoy's. What after-effect did he undergo?

51. "AMOK TIME"

1. Where was the *Enterprise* going before diverting to Vulcan?

2. What is the Vulcan term meaning "cease and desist"?

3. To what did McCoy compare Spock?

4. What is Plak Tow?

5. Name the drug McCoy gave Kirk to simulate death.

6. Whom did T'Pring choose as her champion?

7. What weapon did Spock use to strangle Kirk?

8. Who is the commander of Sector 9?

9. Do you recall the opening phrase of the Vulcan marriage ceremony?

10. To whom did Spock direct the words, "Having is not as satisfying a thing as wanting"?

52. "WHO MOURNS FOR ADONAIS?"

1. Who is the A-and-A officer in the landing party on Pollux IV?

2. Name Apollo's mother and father.

3. Who fell in love with Apollo?

4. What did the other Gods die of?

5. Besides Spock, who else was at the library-computer station?

6. What is Apollo's purpose for the humans?

7. What does A-and-A mean?

8. With what ancient God did Apollo compare Spock?

9. What *Enterprise* crew member is interested romantically in Lt. Palamas?

10. How does Apollo die?

53. "THE CHANGELING"

1. What was the *Nomad*'s first message to the *Enterprise* after its initial attack?

2. What year was the original *Nomad* launched?

3. Who does *Nomad* mistake Captain Kirk ("the Kirk") for?

4. With what space probe did the *Nomad* link forces?

5. What is the new *Nomad*'s purpose?

6. Name the group of planets destroyed by *Nomad* for reasons of imperfection.

7. How does *Nomad* refer to *Tan Ru?*

8. Who was the high-ranking Federation science officer destroyed by *Nomad*?

9. What does *Nomad* do to Lt. Uhura?

10. How is *Nomad* destroyed?

54. "MIRROR, MIRROR"

1. What does Kirk want from the Halkans?

2. Who is the head of the Halkan council?

3. What causes the transporter malfunction that throws the landing party into an alternate universe?

4. In the alternate universe, who is Kirk's bodyguard?

5. What were the prefix initials on the alternate *Enterprise*, and what did they stand for?

6. Where did Marlena Moreau work aboard the *Enterprise?*

7. Who would be glad to have Marlena-2, if Kirk-2 rejects her?

8. In the alternate universe, what is Kirk's secret weapon?

9. How did Kirk-2 gain control of the U.S.S. *Enterprise?*

10. What is Chekov-2's punishment for attempting to assassinate Kirk-2?

55. "THE APPLE"

1. With what does Sayana gift Mr. Spock?

2. How is Hendorff killed?

3. Who is killed by a lightning bolt?

4. What antidote does Spock assimilate in order to reverse the fatal effects the pod plant could have had on his body?

5. What did Ensign Mallory's father do for Kirk?

6. From what couple did Makora and Sayana learn the expression of affection known to Terrans as kissing?

7. Who is "the Eyes of God"?

8. How many credits are invested in Spock?

9. Name the group responsible for feeding the computer its needed organic materials.

10. What does the computer's aboveground outlet resemble?

56. "THE DOOMSDAY MACHINE"

1. What is the name of Commodore Matt Decker's starship?

2. What young *Enterprise* engineering technician accompanied the boarding party?

3. On what planet did the crew of the *Constellation* attempt to take refuge?

4. The berserker "eats" planets with what type of energy force beam?

5. Where is the berserker headed?

6. According to Spock, what are their chances for deactivating it?

7. Whom did Spock order to "escort" Decker to Sick Bay?

8. What material is the hull of the "doomsday machine" made of?

9. How is Decker killed?

10. How does Kirk destroy the machine?

57. "CATSPAW"

1. From what source does Sylvia reap her powers?

2. In this episode Kyle had only two words to speak. Name them.

3. What was Kirk's term for Korob's magic?

4. Who was left in charge of the *Enterprise* when Kirk, Spock, and McCoy transported to Pyris VII?

5. What four types of precious gems did Korob offer Kirk if he would leave the planet?

6. What were Scotty's only two words in the episode?

7. Why were Sylvia and Korob on Pyris VII?

8. What type of occult paraphernalia disguises Korob's transmuter?

9. Whom did Sylvia refer to as being clever, resourceful, and handsome?

10. How did Sylvia kill Korob?

58. "I, MUDD"

1. Which android had no duplicate?

2. How many days did it take to get to Mudd's planet?

3. Exactly how many androids were on Mudd's planet?

4. How long was Norman aboard the *Enterprise* before he took over?

5. Which Alice did Spock say he loved?

6. How many times was the line, "I am not programmed to respond in that area" spoken?

7. What are the four named methods of execution on Deneb V?

8. What was the first name of the male androids?

9. Who was on duty in the Auxiliary Control Room when Norman took over?

10. What tune does McCoy hum to puzzle the Alice androids?

59. "METAMORPHOSIS"

1. To what planet is Nancy Hedford dispatched to stop a war?

2. With what disease does Nancy become infected?

3. How old was Cochrane when the Companion found him?

4. Why did the Companion draw the *Galileo* to Gamma Canaris N?

5. Where were Kirk and Spock escorting the ill Nancy for treatment before being diverted?

6. What major discovery by Cochrane enables starships to exist?

7. According to McCoy, how many years ago did Cochrane supposedly die?

8. Why does the cloud want to keep Cochrane on Gamma Canaris N?

9. How is Nancy saved?

10. What type of energy does the cloud possess?

60. "JOURNEY TO BABEL"

1. Why has there been silence between Spock and Sarek for eighteen years?

2. What subject is destined to be the most volatile at the Babel Conference?

3. Who murders Gav the Tellarite?

4. McCoy wished to use an experimental drug on Spock but it would put undue strain on what two vital organs?

5. What weapon does Thelev wound Kirk with?

6. By what percentage did Spock's blood-production rate increase after he took the experimental drug?

7. What was used to revive Sarek's heart after it had stopped?

8. By what means was Sarek accused of murdering Gav?

9. How did Thelev signal the trailing spacecraft?

10. How long will Kirk be in Sick Bay if he cooperates with McCoy?

61. "FRIDAY'S CHILD"

1. What is the name of the crewman who was killed as the landing party beamed down?

2. From what two Klingon ships did the *Enterprise* receive distress signals?

3. How many tribes on Capella IV?

4. What mineral did the Federation wish to mine on Capella IV?

5. What did McCoy do when Eleen slapped him for touching her?

6. What was Scott's reply when the Klingons sent the second distress signal?

7. What did Kirk use to start a fire in the cave?

8. Name the Capellan weapon.

9. Identify Eleen's son.

10. Who finally kills the Klingon agent?

62. "THE DEADLY YEARS"

1. Who on board the *Enterprise* will soon be the Commander of Starbase 10?

2. What was the name of the dead man Chekov discovered?

3. What were the names of the elderly couple, seen in the beginning, who died later?

4. What planet is the *Enterprise* investigating?

5. When Captain Kirk started aging, what was the first order he found himself repeating?

6. At what rate did Spock, Kirk, McCoy, and Galway age each day?

7. How long had it been since Kirk had seen Dr. Janet Wallace?

8. What was the only communication between Janet and Jim during their time apart?

9. What communication code had the Romulans broken?

10. Why didn't Chekov, who was also part of the landing party, contract the aging disease?

63. "OBSESSION"

1. Who was the Captain of the U.S.S. *Farragut* when the cloud creature was encountered?

2. How did the cloud kill its victims?

3. What planet is awaiting the medical shipments from the *Enterprise*?

4. According to Kirk, what inner feeling was recognized as a command prerogative?

5. Name the planet that was home to the cloud.

6. What did the cloud smell similar to?

7. How does the cloud gain entrance to the *Enterprise*?

8. Why does the cloud turn back after entering the *Enterprise*?

9. Who accompanies Kirk in luring the cloud into the trap?

10. With what is the cloud destroyed?

64. "WOLF IN THE FOLD"

1. How did the people of Argelian show their approval for performers?

2. What part of Scotland does Scotty recall in his conversation with Kara?

3. What is Scott found holding over the dead body of Kara?

4. Administrator Hengist is not originally from Argelian. From what planet does he hail?

5. Who is Jaris's wife who possesses empathetic contact powers?

6. What type of tricorder reading was ordered for Scott?

7. What earth criminal is the entity compared to?

8. Name the city on earth where five women were knifed in 1974.

9. Dr. McCoy's tranquilizers were so powerful that they could even calm what type of natural disaster?

10. What emotion does the entity thrive on?

65. "THE TROUBLE WITH TRIBBLES"

1. What signal does Space Station K-7 send to the *Enterprise*?

2. For what planet is the quadrotriticale grain, being held aboard the Space Station K-7, intended?

3. Who gets credit for starting all the trouble with the tribbles?

4. How did the tribbles spread throughout the *Enterprise*?

5. How did Uhura get her tribble?

6. To whom did Uhura, in turn, give a tribble?

7. How many tribbles did Kirk count in Sick Bay?

8. Who thought of giving the tribbles to the Klingons?

9. What did Spock compare a tribble to?

10. Besides Antarean glow water, what else did the peddler attempt to sell?

66. "THE GAMESTERS OF TRISKELION"

1. What three crew members of the *Enterprise* are snatched to Triskelion?

2. Who is the head thrall on the planet?

3. What brings great pain to the Terrans when they disobey the Triskelions?

4. How long was the rest period during the fight between Kirk and Kloog?

5. What is Triskelion "money" called?

6. Who is Kirk's thrall?

7. How many Providers are there?

8. Who replaced Chekov as Navigator?

9. How many thralls will Kirk have to defeat in order to free himself, his fellow crewmen, and the thralls?

10. Who was Chekov's thrall?

67. "A PIECE OF THE ACTION"

1. What is the name of the planet whose civilization resembles that of Chicago in the 1920's?

2. What ship originally contaminated the planet?

3. Where did Bela Oxmyx suggest the landing party beam down, and when?

4. What popular twentieth-century game do Oxmyx and Kirk play during their first meeting?

5. Give the title of the book by which Iotians lead their lives.

6. What fictional card game does Kirk teach the guards?

7. Who is Oxmyx's right-hand man?

8. What territory does Jojo Kraco rule?

9. Kirk and Spock enlist the services of a young boy to gain entrance to the Southside headquarters. What does the youngster ask in return?

10. What percent of the total "cut" will the Federation receive?

68. "THE IMMUNITY SYNDROME"

1. How many Vulcans were aboard the *Intrepid*?

2. According to Spock, what emotion did the Vulcan crew feel as they were being destroyed?

3. What actually destroyed the *Intrepid*?

4. Who was Commander of the *Intrepid*?

5. Where was the *Enterprise* headed before going to investigate Sector 39J?

6. How does Spock plan to destroy the amoeba?

7. What does the mammoth amoeba consider the *Enterprise* to be, thus warranting its destruction?

8. What type of recorder did Spock take with him to scan the amoeba?

9. How many levers did Spock pull to reduce his life support systems in the shuttlecraft?

10. Who received the stimulant shots on the bridge?

69. "A PRIVATE LITTLE WAR"

1. How many times did Chapel have to hit Spock before he regained consciousness?

2. What was the "people's exhibit #1"?

3. Name the type of animal which bites Kirk.

4. Who treats Kirk's infliction?

5. Who treats Spock's wound?

6. How many flintlocks did Kirk tell Scotty to make?

7. What was used as an antidote for the Mugato poisoning?

8. Which villager is offered a governorship in the Klingon Empire?

9. Whom has Kirk known on the planet for thirteen years?

10. What is Nona offering to the natives when they kill her?

70. "RETURN TO TOMORROW"

1. What type of scientist is Anne Mulhall?

2. Name the planet on which the "entities" were found.

3. How many "receptacles" had malfunctions?

4. How long had Thalassa, Sargon, and Henoch spent in the receptacles?

5. Whose body does Henoch inhabit?

6. How long did Henoch say an android robot body would last?

7. What was Kirk's body temperature when Sargon first tried to inhabit it?

8. Where are the intellects of Kirk, Mulhall, and Spock kept while their bodies are on loan?

9. Who unknowingly administered the wrong medication to Kirk?

10. What was to be injected at the rate of 10cc's an hour to Kirk, Spock, and Ann?

71. "PATTERNS OF FORCE"

1. What weapon attacked the *Enterprise*?

2. Who was sent as a cultural observer to Ekos and also was once one of Kirk's instructors at the Space Academy?

3. What is the purpose of a subcutaneous transponder?

4. Who was the "Hero of the Fatherland" seen in the televised bulletin, and what award was she presented?

5. Who was Uletta?

6. What does Spock use to construct a crude phaser?

7. Who murders Gill, and with what weapon?

8. What rank was on the uniform McCoy wore?

9. Who kills Melakon?

10. After the fall of Melakon's neo-Nazi regime, who is chosen to lead the cultures into a peaceful coexistence?

72. "BY ANY OTHER NAME"

1. What Kelvan took charge of the *Enterprise*'s engineering section?

2. How is Yeoman Thompson killed?

3. How long will it take the *Enterprise* to transport the Kelvans back to Andromeda?

4. What disease did McCoy tell Tomar that Spock had suffered from some ten years ago?

5. What drug, disguised as vitamins, is administered to Hanar?

6. To whom does Kirk introduce kissing?

7. What planet did Scotty's green drink come from?

8. Who becomes jealous of Kirk's amorous methods?

9. How do the Kelvans, in their true form, appear to Spock?

10. What planet will the Kelvans most likely colonize?

73. "THE OMEGA GLORY"

1. To what section of the *Exeter* did the *Enterprise* landing party beam?

2. Name the *Enterprise* security guard killed by Tracey.

3. What do the Yangs call their worn American flag?

4. How did Tracey escape death from the virus?

5. What did the Omegans call the phasers?

6. Who was about to decapitate Cloud William and Sirah when Kirk interrupted?

7. How many shuttlecraft on the *Exeter*?

8. How many phasers did Tracey ask Kirk to send from the *Enterprise*?

9. What one word saves Kirk from death by Cloud William?

10. From what twentieth-century societies are the Yangs and Kohms descended?

74. "THE ULTIMATE COMPUTER"

1. What two prestigious awards did Dr. Daystrom receive before inventing the M-5?

2. Who was the Captain of the U.S.S. *Excalibur*?

3. Name the ore freighter destroyed by the M-5.

4. How many crewmen died on the *Lexington*?

5. What was Commodore Wesley's nickname for Kirk after the M-5 took over?

6. What class of computer technician is Spock?

7. To whom does Star Fleet grant permission to destroy the M-5?

8. What crime does Kirk convince the M-5 it has committed?

9. What is the name of the green drink that Dr. McCoy is so adept at preparing?

10. What were the M-5's last words before surrendering?

75. "BREAD AND CIRCUSES"

1. What was the name of Captain Merik's ship?

2. On what planet does this episode take place?

3. Who is now First Citizen of the Empire?

4. What message was sent to Scotty by Kirk after Spock, McCoy, and he were taken prisoner?

5. Though the planet is similar to twentieth-century earth in appearance and technology, what culture does it resemble?

6. Name the title of the television program which is featuring a gladiator fight with Kirk, Spock, and McCoy.

7. What products are advertised on the television program?

8. Who is McCoy to battle?

9. With what weapon does Proconsul Claudius Marcus slay Captain Merik?

10. What Terran religion parallels that of the sun worshippers on Planet 892-IV?

76. "ASSIGNMENT: EARTH"

1. From what military base was the nuclear device launched?

2. What was Gary Seven's official title?

3. On what road were agents 201 and 347 killed?

4. Who was Launch Director of the rocket base?

5. Where did Gary Seven plan to blow up the orbital bomb?

6. Who was Gary's secretary?

7. To whom were Spock and Kirk taken when they were captured on the base?

8. Who seized them?

9. What is Gary Seven's address?

10. Name Gary's "cat."

77. "SPOCK'S BRAIN"

1. Who steals Spock's brain?

2. What device does McCoy use to keep Spock's body alive while the search for the brain continues?

3. What do the Eymorgs call the brain?

4. How is the *Enterprise* able to trace Kara and ultimately find the brain?

5. How long can information from the Great Teacher be retained?

6. What instrument keeps the Morgs subservient to the Eymorgs?

7. How many control buttons on a wristlet?

8. What is a transporter on Sigma Draconis called?

9. Because they measure the heartbeat and pulse-rate of an individual, what McCoy apparatus is used as a lie detector?

10. How long was the Controller (a/k/a Spock's brain) to keep the Eymorgs alive?

78. "THE *ENTERPRISE* INCIDENT"

1. How many Romulan ships have surrounded the *Enterprise*?

2. Name the Romulan subcommander.

3. To what deck was the female Romulan commander confined?

4. From their present point of space, how long would a subspace message take to reach Starfleet Command?

5. Kirk told the Romulan Commander that the *Enterprise* was due for an overhaul. How long ago?

6. What device did McCoy use to revive Kirk from the Vulcan death grip?

7. What ploy did Spock use to delay his execution?

8. What is the Romulan device which renders its ship invisible?

9. What is the equivalent name for a Romulan bridge?

10. Who is accidentally beamed aboard with Spock?

79. "THE PARADISE SYNDROME"

1. What does McCoy first smell on the earth-like planet?

2. What mixture are the Indians who inhabit the planet?

3. What was the purpose of the *Enterprise* visit?

4. What does Spock use to demonstrate why the *Enterprise* must leave the planet and divert the asteroid?

5. Name the Indian medicine man.

6. What feat establishes Kirk as a God?

7. Why doesn't Salish know the secret of the temple?

8. Who becomes Kirk's wife?

9. What race established the planet, the Indians, and the obelisk?

10. How is the door of the obelisk opened?

80. "AND THE CHILDREN SHALL LEAD"

1. Name the poison that the Starnes Expedition administered to themselves.

2. How many stars on the Federation flag?

3. When the children were choosing ice cream, what was Steve's first choice?

4. From what disease did Dr. McCoy first suggest the children were suffering?

5. Where was Gorgan preserved until the Starnes Expedition uncovered him?

6. Which child wore her hair in pigtails?

7. What planet did Gorgan wish to conquer before overtaking the galaxy?

8. Who was responsible for discovering Gorgan?

9. By what name do the children refer to Gorgan?

10. Where are the children finally taken for therapy?

81. "IS THERE IN TRUTH NO BEAUTY?

1. What drink was served at the dinner for Miranda?

2. What is a sensor web?

3. What must be worn to prevent insanity at the sight of a Medusan?

4. Do you recall Marvick's last words before his death?

5. Name the poet whose work Spock recites while in mind link with Kollos.

6. What is the section of the *Enterprise* where flowers and plants are kept?

7. What does IDIC stand for?

8. Which Shakespearean play does Spock quote from while having the link with Kollos?

9. What warp factor must be surpassed when a space time continuum begins?

10. Who restores Spock's sanity?

82. "SPECTRE OF THE GUN"

1. What is the date of the gunfight at the O.K. Corral?

2. At what time is the Clanton gang supposed to die?

3. Which Earp called Kirk yellow?

4. What were the only two drinks available from Ed?

5. With whom does Chekov fall in love?

6. Who is the sheriff of Cochise County?

7. Who is "the man who kills on sight"?

8. What name brand of alcoholic beverage did McCoy use to clean Kirk's wound?

9. How does Spock convince the others of the illusion?

10. What was the purpose of the mission?

83. "DAY OF THE DOVE"

1. How long have the Klingons and the Federation been at peace until this incident?

2. Which of the landing party is cruelly tortured?

3. Who is Kang's wife?

4. To whom does Captain Kirk give command of the Engineering and Control?

5. What does Scotty call Kang after the Klingon cuts off their life-support systems?

6. On what does the alien life form exist?

7. Name the method used to place Kirk and Mara in the Engineering Room.

8. What crude weapons does the alien provide for the battle between *Enterprise* crewmen and Klingons?

9. Who attacks Mara?

10. How long will the war between the Federation and the Klingons continue if the alien has its way?

84. "FOR THE WORLD IS HOLLOW AND I HAVE TOUCHED THE SKY"

1. Dr. McCoy has only one year to live. What must he have for a cure?

2. When Spock, McCoy, and Kirk beam aboard the asteroid, who greets them?

3. In a touching moment, Dr. McCoy confesses that he has lived what kind of life?

4. The asteroid is discovered to actually be a nuclear-powered spaceship heading toward a green world. How long has it been traveling?

5. From what planet was the ship dispatched?

6. If McCoy is to become one of Natira's people, what must he have implanted in his face?

7. What part of the oracle does Kirk press to open the entrance to the Instrument Room?

8. What has caused the ship to be on a collision course with Daran V?

9. What disease does McCoy have?

10. Where is a cure for "Bones" finally found?

85. "THE THOLIAN WEB"

1. What was the name of the missing ship?

2. How long has the ship been missing?

3. Who handled the transporter when Kirk, Spock, McCoy, and Chekov beamed aboard?

4. After the Captain was initially lost, how much time elapsed until the next interphase?

5. What were the words on Kirk's "last orders" tape?

6. Name the Tholian commander.

7. What cure did McCoy find for space madness?

8. With what substance did McCoy mix the space madness cure?

9. What did the Tholians call the region of space warp?

10. When was the *Defiant* seen again?

86. "PLATO'S STEPCHILDREN"

1. Who is the King of Platonius?

2. Who is the court jester?

3. What special type of powers do these Platonians possess?

4. Parmen offers the *Enterprise* officers special gifts in forgiveness. What is McCoy given?

5. What chemical provides the Platonians with their powers?

6. What two female crew members are brought to the planet by Parmen?

7. Can you recall Captain Kirk's words when he saw the two females being drawn into Parmen's quarters?

8. Why is Alexander devoid of the psychokinesis?

9. What song does Spock sing for the Platonians?

10. Who is Parmen's wife?

87. "WINK OF AN EYE"

1. How did Spock deduce that the Scalos inhabitants were humanoid in appearance?

2. When the landing party arrived on Scalos, what crewman was the first to disappear?

3. Name the process by which Kirk disappears.

4. What does Kirk's voice sound like to the crewmen of the *Enterprise* after he has vanished?

5. Why is Kirk's phaser ineffective on Deela?

6. Besides Kirk, who admitted to drinking contaminated coffee?

7. What natural disaster had caused the strange conditions on Scalos?

8. What purpose were the men of the *Enterprise* to serve to the Scalosian women?

9. Who becomes jealous of Deela's affections for Kirk?

10. Why does Spock remain accelerated after a cure has long been found?

88. "THE EMPATH"

1. Name the star about to nova.

2. Who names Gem?

3. What creatures inhabiting the planet appear as rock formations?

4. In what chapter of the Bible is the verse quoted by Dr. Ozaba found?

5. By what means did Kirk, Spock, and McCoy gain entrance to the cavern inhabited by Gem?

6. Name two scientists who died as Gem attempted to exercise his empathetic abilities.

7. According to Vians, who is "on schedule"?

8. What kind of damage to Spock's body could occur from the Vians' experiment?

9. Who lives on Gamma Vertis IV?

10. Whose life does Gem save while risking his own?

89. "ELAAN OF TROYIUS"

1. Who was supposed to teach Elaan "civilized" manners?

2. What causes Kirk to become romantically involved with Elaan?

3. Why is Elaan marrying the Troyian leader?

4. Of what precious commodity is Elaan's necklace composed?

5. What antidote does McCoy employ to battle her tears?

6. What type of obsolete hand-artillery do the Elasian guards carry?

7. What planet is Troyius battling?

8. Who gifted Elaan with her wedding gown?

9. What does Elaan call the nodules strung as a necklace?

10. Where is the Number 4 shield located?

90. "WHOM GODS DESTROY"

1. How many inmates on Elba II?

2. Captain Garth demanded to be addressed by what title?

3. Where did Garth learn cellular metamorphosis?

4. What were the chess code words Scott was to give Kirk?

5. The rehabilitation chair incorporated the use of what type of sound waves?

6. What title did Garth confer upon Kirk at the coronation?

7. How much of the explosive does Garth use to destroy Marta, his mistress?

8. During the final confrontation when Garth appears as Kirk, what is Garth holding just as Spock stuns him?

9. What was Kirk's proper response to the chess code?

10. What Biblical king did Kirk mention to Spock?

91. "LET THAT BE YOUR LAST BATTLEFIELD"

1. From what Starbase was the shuttlecraft reported stolen?

2. How long has the craft been missing?

3. How many years had Bele been chasing after Lokai?

4. Which side of Lokai's body is black?

5. Why was the *Enterprise* on its way to Ariannus?

6. What two systems of the *Enterprise* did Bele burn out?

7. How many times was the *Enterprise* able to spray Ariannus?

8. When Bele finally returns to Cheron, how many inhabitants are left?

9. How are Bele and Lokai able to protect themselves from phaser fire?

10. How did the inhabitants of Cheron die?

92. "THE MARK OF GIDEON"

1. What disease is Kirk carrying that Odona is to contract and spread to Gideon?

2. Name the Star Fleet official who became Spock's nemesis.

3. Why does Odona need to infect her planet with a deadly virus?

4. Why does Kirk have a bruise on his arm?

5. Who proves to Spock that the transporter is working properly?

6. What is missing from the *Enterprise* replica that the Gideons assembled?

7. According to McCoy, what was "the worst possible decision" Spock could make?

8. How many years will the *Enterprise*'s food supply last?

9. What relation is Odona to Hodin?

10. Who rescues Kirk and Odona?

93. "THAT WHICH SURVIVES"

1. Name the *Enterprise* geologist killed in this episode.

2. Who was the first person killed by Losira?

3. Who takes Sulu's position when he is with the landing party?

4. How far did Losira claim she flung the *Enterprise* from its original position?

5. How does Losira kill her victims?

6. What does the phaser do to the planet surface when Kirk attempts to dig a grave for D'Amato?

7. When Losira sets out for Sulu, how do Kirk and McCoy stop her?

8. What incredible speed does the *Enterprise* reach when its matter-antimatter controls are fused together?

9. Who risks his life to stop the increasing speed of the *Enterprise*?

10. What actually controls the actions of Losira?

94. "THE LIGHTS OF ZETAR"

1. What is Mira Romaine's initial assignment for the Federation?

2. Where was Mira born?

3. Who falls in love with her?

4. What are Mira's parents' first names?

5. What medical tests did McCoy give Mira after the phasers hit the "lights"?

6. What condition did the *Enterprise* attain after the "lights" invaded?

7. At what warp factor did Sulu say the "lights" traveled?

8. How many distinct life units made up the "lights"?

9. What was Mira's father's past profession?

10. How is Mira ridded of the "lights"?

95. "REQUIEM FOR METHUSELAH"

1. What is the only known cure for Rigellian fever?

2. Spock played a sonata by what composer?

3. What three great earth minds did Flint know personally?

4. Under what alias did Flint purchase Holberg 917G?

5. What scientific subject did Reena wish to discuss with Spock?

6. Where was Flint born?

7. What emotion did Spock feel after witnessing Flint's collection of artwork and books?

8. Who fights with Flint over the affections of Reena?

9. To what Terran disease is Rigellian fever compared?

10. According to McCoy, what emotion is "not written into Spock's book"?

96. "THE WAY TO EDEN"

1. What was Dr. Sevrin's original profession before he started the Eden movement?

2. What ability did Tongo Rad inherit from his father?

3. What is Tongo Rad's favorite hobby?

4. What common Terran food is used by the "space hippies" as a symbol of their cause?

5. Who was the first to eat the fruit and die?

6. Name the spaceship that the "space hippies" are using to search for Eden.

7. Who particularly empathizes with the Eden-seekers?

8. Who tries to enlist Sulu in the cause?

9. Who carries Sythococcus novae?

10. What color was the deadly fruit?

97. "THE CLOUD MINERS"

1. Because of the zienite gas poisoning, the "intellect reading" of the Troglytes was reduced by what percentage?

2. What Federation branch would serve as mediator between the miners and Council?

3. How many containers of zienite were beamed to the *Enterprise*?

4. What are the Troglyte guards called?

5. How does Kirk convince Vanna of the gas's ill effects?

6. When the Troglyte was apprehended in Stratos without his transport card, what excuse did he give Plasus for being there?

7. What are the "gas masks" called?

8. Where is Vanna taken for punishment?

9. What tool is used to mine zienite?

10. Why did the *Enterprise* want the zienite?

98. "THE SAVAGE CURTAIN"

1. What thought-impossible life form was detected on the planet?

2. How large was the Earth-like area of the planet?

3. Who is to guard Lincoln with a phaser?

4. When Yarnek stops the engines, how long will it be before the ship explodes?

5. To what historical character did Lincoln compare Kirk?

6. Who led a deadly genocidal war on Earth in the twenty-first century?

7. From what planet did Yarnek hail?

8. Who flees with Genghis Khan?

9. What obsolete term did Lincoln use when he greeted Uhura?

10. Who destroys Lincoln?

99. "ALL OUR YESTERDAYS"

1. What star is about to nova?

2. Who is the last inhabitant of Sarpeidon?

3. What is the name of the time travel device?

4. Whom does Spock grow fond of when McCoy and he are thrown into the planet's ice age?

5. What is the purpose of the carrell?

6. What medication is used for McCoy's frostbite?

7. Do you recall the slang word for a pickpocket in Kirk's time of Charles II?

8. What did Zarabeth offer Spock to eat?

9. Who placed Zarabeth in the ice age?

10. How many tapes are in the library?

100. "TURNABOUT INTRUDER"

1. With what starship was the *Enterprise* to rendevous at Beta Aurigae?

2. How long were Kirk and Lester together at the Academy?

3. What killed Dr. Lester's staff?

4. What does Janice promise Coleman if he assists her?

5. When Janice is inside Kirk's body, what does she accuse Spock, McCoy, and Scotty of attempting?

6. Where does Spock suggest that Dr. Lester/Kirk be taken for extensive medical treatment?

7. Who was the communications officer that Janice, in Kirk's body, mistakenly called Lisa?

8. What were the scientists doing on Camus II before their death?

9. Why was Coleman relieved of his post as the ship's Medical Officer?

10. Why did Coleman stay with Janice after her collapse?

ANSWERS

QUIZ 1

1. September 8, 1966
2. NBC-TV
3. President of Desilu Productions, original producer of *Star Trek*
4. Chekov, played by Walter Koenig
5. San Francisco Navy Yard
6. Georgia
7. Mark Leonard and Jane Wyatt
8. Salt shakers
9. The Jefferies Tube
10. Swahili for "freedom"

QUIZ 2

1. Uhura; "Man Trap"
2. McCoy; "City on the Edge of Forever"
3. Kirk; "Whom Gods Destroy"
4. McCoy; "Journey to Babel"
5. Scott; "The Trouble with Tribbles"
6. Kirk; "City on the Edge of Forever"
7. Kirk; "Tomorrow is Yesterday"
8. McCoy; "Operation—Annihilate!"
9. McCoy; "Amok Time"
10. Kirk; "This Side of Paradise"

QUIZ 3

1. "The Trouble with Tribbles"
2. "The Man Trap"
3. "A Piece of the Action"
4. "Journey to Babel"
5. "Metamorphosis"
6. "I, Mudd"
7. "The Mark of Gideon"
8. "Spectre of the Gun"
9. "Amok Time"
10. "Turnabout Intruder"

QUIZ 4

1. Blue
2. M'Umbha
3. "The Conscience of the King," "Charlie X," and "The Changeling"
4. Dr. Piper
5. "Mirror, Mirror" and "The Menagerie"
6. Warp 3
7. "Spock's Brain"
8. Sulu
9. Trelane (in "The Squire of Gothos")
10. Triskelion

QUIZ 5

1. a
2. i
3. d
4. g
5. h
6. b
7. f
8. j
9. c
10. e

QUIZ 6

1. "Errand of Mercy"
2. "Dagger of the Mind"
3. "Shore Leave"
4. "Arena"
5. "The Man Trap"
6. "The Doomsday Machine"
7. "For the World is Hollow and I Have Touched the Sky"
8. "The Tholian Web"
9. "The Paradise Syndrome"
10. "A Private Little War"

QUIZ 7

1. Surgo-op
2. *Copernicus*
3. Dramia II
4. Fruit
5. Phylos
6. Villi
7. Lt. Uhura
8. "The Magicks of Megas-tu"
9. *Devisor*
10. "The Counter-Clock Incident"

QUIZ 8

1. Iowa
2. Sam Kirk
3. SC937-0176 CEC
4. Captain Christopher Pike
5. Fifth
6. Abraham Lincoln
7. Seventeen years old
8. Dr. Janet Wallace
9. "Plato's Stepchildren"
10. Ruth

QUIZ 9

1. "Charlie X"
2. "Whom Gods Destroy"
3. "And the Children Shall Lead"
4. "The Omega Glory"
5. "Wolf in the Fold"
6. "What Are Little Girls Made Of?"
7. "The Empath"
8. "The Way to Eden"
9. "The Cloud Miners"
10. "The Mark of Gideon"

QUIZ 10

1. "A Piece of the Action"
2. "Arena"
3. "Wink of an Eye"
4. "Day of the Dove"
5. "The Tholian Web"
6. "The Ultimate Computer"
7. "The *Enterprise* Incident"
8. "Bread and Circuses"
9. "Operation—Annihilate!"
10. "A Taste of Armageddon"

QUIZ 11

1. c
2. a
3. e
4. d
5. j
6. b
7. h
8. g
9. i
10. f

QUIZ 12

1. Seventh
2. Command, Engineering, and Science and Ships Services
3. Six
4. Twelve
5. *Galileo*
6. "Mirror, Mirror"
7. Eighteen
8. Walter M. Jefferies
9. Nine hundred and forty-seven feet
10. Four hundred and twenty-eight

QUIZ 13

1. Father—Sarek
2. Library-Computer station
3. Vulcans have pointed ears to "capture" sound waves in the thin atmosphere of planet Vulcan
4. Green
5. Thirteen years
6. Two hundred and fifty years
7. School teacher
8. In the lower right area of his chest
9. Scientist
10. None

QUIZ 14

1. c
2. g
3. i
4. a
5. j
6. f
7. d
8. e
9. h
10. b

QUIZ 15

1. Writer David Gerrold
2. "The Cage"
3. "Turnabout Intruder"
4. Five years
5. Twenty-third
6. Vulcan harp
7. Sonic disrupter pistol
8. Joanna
9. Seven
10. Top of right shoulder

QUIZ 16

1. A portable sensor-computer-recorder
2. "Miri"
3. Red
4. "The Menagerie"
5. Scotty
6. Pavel
7. Charlie Evans
8. The Navigator (Chekov) and Helmsman (Sulu)
9. None
10. Those with conditions resembling Earth

QUIZ 17

1. e
2. g
3. a
4. i
5. h
6. j
7. f
8. b
9. c
10. d

QUIZ 18

1. McCoy to Kirk; "Elaan of Troyius"
2. Yeoman Rand to the salt/vampire monster appearing as Crewman Green; "The Man Trap"
3. Harry Mudd to Kirk; "I, Mudd"
4. Spock to Maximus Flavius; "Bread and Circuses"
5. Lokai to Kirk; "Let This Be Your Last Battlefield"
6. Vina to Captain Pike; "The Menagerie"
7. Kor to Kirk; "Errand of Mercy"
8. Flint to Kirk; "Requiem for Methuselah"
9. Kirk to Charlie; "Charlie X"
10. McCoy to Kirk; "The Paradise Syndrome"

QUIZ 19

1. "The Man Trap"
2. "Space, the final frontier . . ."
3. "Errand of Mercy"
4. "Dagger of the Mind"
5. "Amok Time"
6. Lt. Uhura
7. "Where No Man Has Gone Before"
8. Montgomery
9. "Is There In Truth No Beauty?"
10. "Plato's Stepchildren"

QUIZ 20

1. d; Skip Homeier
2. e; Vic Perrin
3. c; Diana Muldaur
4. h; Michael Zaslow
5. i; Abraham Sofaer
6. j; Stewart Moss
7. g; Morgan Woodward
8. b; Jay Jones
9. f; Sean Morgan
10. a; Paul Baxley

QUIZ 21

1. Harry Mudd
2. Captain Christopher
3. Jojo Kraco
4. Samuel T. Cogley
5. Lt. Maria McGivers
6. Edith Keeler
7. Losira
8. Cyrano Jones
9. Lord Petri
10. Aurelan Kirk
11. Natira

QUIZ 22

1. To give annual medical examinations
2. A girl he had met on Wrigley's Pleasure planet
3. Borgia root poison
4. Plum
5. Crewman Green
6. The alien plant attracted to Yeoman Rand
7. Cry
8. Commander José Domingues
9. Passenger pigeons and buffalo
10. Sodium chloride (salt)

QUIZ 23

1. Seventeen (Terran years)
2. Thasus
3. U.S.S. *Antares*
4. In a colonizing expedition crash
5. Yeoman Rand
6. Three
7. Turkeys
8. Colony 5
9. Captain Kirk
10. Turned her into a lizard

QUIZ 24

1. Its own captain
2. Materializer
3. A red glow in his eyes
4. Delta Vega
5. Kirk once taught Mitchell at Star Fleet Academy
6. Uses his powers to cause a cable to strangle him
7. Dr. Elizabeth Dehner
8. A phaser rifle
9. By causing a pile of boulders to fall on the Captain
10. "God forgive me."

QUIZ 25

1. Psi 2000
2. Joe Tormolen; depression
3. "Love Mankind" and "Sinner Repent"
4. Through human perspiration
5. He believes Spock is Richelieu and attempts an attack with a fencing foil
6. Cries over his mother
7. Engine room
8. Spock
9. Ten thousand to one
10. The ship's bowling alley

QUIZ 26

1. Technician Fisher
2. Deck 12, Room 3C-46
3. Synchronic meter
4. Ore
5. Technician Wilson
6. Minus 250 degrees Fahrenheit
7. Four
8. Hostility, lust, and violence
9. Compassion, love, and tenderness
10. Transporter unit ionizer

QUIZ 27

1. Ruth Bonaventure, Magda Kovas, and Eve McHuron
2. Smuggling, transporting stolen goods, and purchasing a spaceship with counterfeit money
3. Psychiatric treatment
4. Scotty
5. It was pelagic (no land, covered with water)
6. Two
7. Six
8. Double-jack
9. Red
10. Ben Childress

QUIZ 28

1. Minus 100 degrees Fahrenheit
2. Two
3. Dr. Brown
4. Research biologist
5. Earth Colony 2
6. The "Old Ones"
7. Andrea
8. His body was damaged by the freezing conditions on Exo III
9. Ruk pushed him into a bottomless pit
10. By studying the ruins of Orion

QUIZ 29

1. Life Prolongation Project
2. They aged only one month for every one hundred years
3. Upon entering puberty
4. The children's slang for "grown-up"
5. Biocomputer and portable electron microscope
6. A piano
7. Boxes
8. Jahn
9. She grew jealous of the affections Kirk paid to Yeoman Rand
10. Onlies

QUIZ 30

1. Tantalus V
2. McCoy's
3. "Caution: Infra-sensor Drugs"
4. Triple dose
5. Ensign Berkeley
6. Neural neutralizer
7. Hunger
8. Through the air conditioning vents
9. Spock, using the Vulcan mind touch
10. He falls into the path of the neutralizer, draining his brain which causes his demise

QUIZ 31

1. To obtain his quarterly physical examination
2. Adrenal gland
3. Spock
4. Dietary salad
5. *Fesarius*
6. Navigator
7. Ten minutes
8. His father
9. Cultural Envoy
10. Tranya

QUIZ 32

1. He was inspecting a Class J starship when the baffle plates erupted
2. Death
3. Commodore José I. Mendez
4. Duranium
5. Lt. Hansen
6. Eleven
7. *Columbia*
8. Vega IX
9. Delta rays
10. Lt. Helen Johanssen

QUIZ 33

1. Three
2. They proved to be too violent to be useful
3. Without the illusion the Talosians created for her, she would be old and crippled
4. Tango
5. Force chamber explosion
6. A mace
7. To distract Kirk
8. Orion
9. Magistrate
10. Star Fleet Command

QUIZ 34

1. Tarsus IV; because of a food drought
2. Caesar of the Stars
3. *Macbeth*
4. "Beyond *Antares*"
5. Tetralubisol
6. *Astral Queen*
7. "Worlds may change, galaxies may change, but a woman remains a woman"
8. He blocks the phaser fire Lenore directs at Kirk
9. She goes insane
10. Galactic Cultural Exchange Project

QUIZ 35

1. Marrying Angela Martine and Robert Tomlinson
2. To guard the neutral zone between Federation and Romulan territories
3. Praetor
4. Romii
5. Commander Hanson
6. Their invisibility screen worked both ways, causing a reflection
7. Icarus 4
8. Decius
9. Robert Tomlinson
10. Spock saved his life

QUIZ 36

1. Omicron Delta region
2. Yeoman Barrows
3. The starboard section
4. The Black Knight
5. Ruth
6. Rigel II
7. Don Juan
8. Finnegan
9. Samurai warrior
10. Grumman Hellcat

QUIZ 37

1. Commissioner Ferris
2. Murasaki 312
3. Gaetano and Latimer
4. Taurus II
5. Lt. Boma
6. Folsom Point
7. Five hundred
8. New Paris
9. Six minutes
10. To ignite them as a distress signal

QUIZ 38

1. Lt. DeSalle
2. Yeoman Ross
3. Star desert
4. Treason, conspiracy, and insurrection
5. Three
6. Lt. Karl Jaeger
7. Uhura
8. Beta 6
9. Trelane's parents stop him from further harm
10. "I would've."

QUIZ 39

1. Commodore Travers
2. Lt. O'Herlihy
3. Lieutenant
4. Lt. DePaul
5. Repulsion
6. Diamonds
7. A hand phaser or a good solid club
8. Sulfur, potassium nitrate, and coal
9. Cannon
10. A toga

QUIZ 40

1. Bluejay 4 and Blackjack, respectively
2. Little green men
3. The late 1960's
4. Cygnet XIV
5. The computer called Kirk "dear," and, according to Spock, had "an unfortunate tendency to giggle"
6. Colonel Fellini
7. The slingshot effect
8. Shaun Geoffrey Christopher; leader of first Earth-Saturn probe
9. Chicken soup
10. United Earth Space Probe Agency

QUIZ 41

1. Perjury
2. Starbase 11
3. U.S.S. *Intrepid*
4. "Four years, seven months, and an odd number of days"
5. Samuel T. Cogley
6. Five times
7. Books
8. Jamie
9. Corrigan
10. U.S.S. *Republic*

QUIZ 42

1. Lt. O'Neil
2. One hundred years
3. Tula
4. Festival
5. Marplon
6. Six o'clock P.M. on Festival day
7. Bilar
8. Lindstrom
9. Six thousand years
10. The Valley

QUIZ 43

1. S. S. *Botany Bay*
2. Suspended animation
3. Eugenics War
4. Khan Noonian Singh
5. The *Enterprise*'s engineering plans
6. The medical decompression chamber
7. Lieutenant Maria McGivers
8. Order
9. Ceti Alpha V
10. Court-martial or exile with Khan

QUIZ 44

1. Ambassador Robert Fox
2. Mea 3
3. Five hundred years
4. Computers
5. Anan 7
6. Two hours
7. Numbers eleven and twelve
8. "Suicide stations"
9. Captain Kirk
10. U.S.S. *Valiant*

QUIZ 45

1. Berthold rays
2. Seventy-two hours
3. Botanist
4. Elias Sandoval
5. Six years
6. He antagonizes him
7. A dragon
8. The sight of his Medal of Honor
9. Starbase 27
10. He uses sound waves

QUIZ 46

1. To mine pergium
2. Twenty-third
3. With a corrosive acid
4. Horta
5. Chief Engineer Vandenberg
6. "A crime against Nature."
7. Lt. Commander Giotto
8. "No Kill I"
9. Thermoconcrete
10. Spock's pointed ears

QUIZ 47

1. D minus
2. The Chairman of the Council of Elders, Ayelborne
3. By masquerading as a Vulcan merchant
4. Baroner
5. The grim face of the Captain is a contrast to the usual smile of an Organian
6. One thousand Organians will die
7. "Go climb a tree!"
8. Trefayne
9. The weapons are heated to 350 degrees, rendering them useless
10. Friendliness

QUIZ 48

1. Commodore Barstow
2. Four
3. Lt. Masters
4. Time chamber
5. Iron-silica
6. To aid him in tracking down his enemy
7. 98.5 degrees Fahrenheit
8. Their respective universes would be destroyed
9. Lazarus A
10. He was inspecting the magnetic communication satellite

QUIZ 49

1. Cordrazine
2. Kid McCook and Mike Mason
3. Edith Keeler
4. Twenty-one
5. Fifteen cents
6. The Orpheum
7. "Let me help"
8. *The Star-Dispatch*
9. She was destined to organize a peace movement that would delay the U.S. from entering World War II, giving the Nazi regime time to develop their atomic bomb
10. "Goodnight, Sweetheart"

QUIZ 50

1. Deneva
2. Sam (George Samuel Kirk); research biologist
3. Scotty, as an engineering advisor
4. Four
5. Eight months
6. "Don't let them go any further"
7. Spinal cord
8. Brain
9. Whether or not to kill the entire population of the planet in order to stop the creatures
10. Blindness

QUIZ 51

1. Altair VI, to be a part of the honor guard at the President's inauguration
2. Kroykah
3. A tight-lipped Aldebaran shell mouth
4. A Vulcan term meaning frenzy
5. Neural paralyzer
6. Captain Kirk
7. Ahn-woon
8. Admiral Komack
9. "Kah-if-farr . . ."
10. Stonn

QUIZ 52

1. Lt. Carolyn Palamas
2. Zeus and Leto
3. Lt. Carolyn Palamas
4. Loneliness
5. Lt. Kyle
6. To have them settle on the planet and worship him
7. Archeology-and-Anthropology
8. Pan
9. Scotty
10. He spreads himself upon the wind and disappears

QUIZ 53

1. "U.S.S. *Enterprise,* this is *Nomad.* My mission is nonhostile."
2. 2002
3. Its creator, Jackson Roykirk
4. *Tan Ru*
5. To seek out perfect life forms and destroy any imperfect ones
6. Malurian system
7. "The Other"
8. Dr. Manway
9. Erases her memory
10. By realizing its own error in thinking Captain Kirk was "the Kirk," it destroys itself

QUIZ 54

1. Dilithium crystals
2. Tharn
3. An ion storm
4. Farrell
5. I.S.S.; Imperial Star Ship
6. The chemistry lab
7. Commander Kenner
8. Tantalus field
9. He assassinated Captain Christopher Pike
10. Exposure in the agony booth

QUIZ 55

1. A necklace of shells
2. By the poison thorns of the pod plant
3. Kaplan
4. Masiform D
5. He helped him get into the Space Academy
6. Chekov and Landon
7. Akuta
8. 122,220-plus
9. Feeders of Vaal
10. A serpent

QUIZ 56

1. U.S.S. *Constellation*
2. Washburn
3. L374-III
4. Pure anti-proton
5. Toward the Earth's galaxy
6. None
7. Mr. Montgomery
8. Neutronium
9. Attempting to destroy the berserker by piloting a stolen *Enterprise* shuttlecraft into the mouth of the "machine"
10. By causing the *Constellation* to explode inside the berserker

QUIZ 57

1. The transmuter in her amulet
2. "Ready, sir"
3. "Mumbo-jumbo"
4. Assistant Chief Engineer Lt. DeSalle
5. Diamonds, rubies, emeralds, and sapphires
6. "Everything's vanished"
7. To prepare for colonization
8. A wand
9. Captain Kirk
10. She transformed herself into a monstrous black cat and crushed Korob beneath a door

QUIZ 58

1. Norman
2. Four
3. 207,809
4. Seventy-two hours
5. Alice 27
6. Five
7. Death by phaser, gas, electrocution, and hanging
8. Herman
9. Ensign Jordan
10. "The Blue Danube"

QUIZ 59

1. Epsilon Canaris III
2. Sakuro's disease
3. Eighty-seven
4. So Cochrane could have human companions
5. To the *Enterprise*
6. Space warp drive
7. One hundred and fifty
8. "She" is in love with Cochrane
9. The Companion merges with her body
10. Electrical

QUIZ 60

1. Sarek has wished his son to become a scientist instead of joining Star Fleet
2. The possible admittance of Coridan to the Federation
3. Thelev
4. The liver and spleen
5. A knife
6. Two hundred percent
7. Cardiostimulator
8. Tal-shaya
9. From a device inside his antennae
10. Two days

QUIZ 61

1. Lt. Grant
2. U.S.S. *Carolina* and S.S. *Dierdre*
3. Ten
4. Topaline
5. He slapped her back
6. "Fool me once, shame on you; fool me twice, shame on me."
7. Magnesite-nitron tablets
8. Kligat
9. Teer Leonard James Akaar
10. Maab's lieutenant

QUIZ 62

1. Commodore George Stocker
2. Alvin
3. Robert and Elaine Johnson
4. Gamma Hydra IV
5. "Maintain standard orbit"
6. Thirty years
7. "Six years, four months, and an odd number of days"
8. Kirk sent her a stargram at the time of her husband's death
9. Code 2
10. He became so scared on Gamma Hydra IV that his adrenalin level increased and thus protected him

QUIZ 63

1. Captain Garrovick
2. By draining the red blood cells
3. Theta VII
4. Intuition
5. Tycho IV
6. Honey
7. Through Impulse vent 2
8. Its first encounter was with Spock whose blood was hardly what the creature desired
9. Ensign Garrovick
10. A matter-antimatter bomb

QUIZ 64

1. By blinking delight lights
2. Edinburgh
3. A blooded knife
4. Rigel IV
5. Sybo
6. Twenty-four-hour regressive memory check
7. Jack the Ripper
8. Kiev, Russia
9. Volcano
10. Fear

QUIZ 65

1. Priority-1 call
2. Sherman's Planet
3. Cyrano Jones
4. Through the air ducts
5. As a gift from Cyrano Jones
6. Ensign Freeman
7. Eleven
8. Spock
9. An ermine violin
10. Spican flame gems

QUIZ 66

1. Kirk, Chekov, and Uhura
2. Galt
3. The collars
4. Fifteen trisecs
5. Quatloos
6. Shahna
7. Three
8. Ensign Haines
9. Three
10. Tamoon

QUIZ 67

1. Iotia
2. U.S.S. *Horizon*
3. "At the yellow fireplug on the corner . . ."; ". . . in five minutes"
4. Billiards
5. *Chicago Mobs of the Twenties*
6. Fizzbin
7. Kalo
8. Southside territory
9. "A piece of the action"
10. Forty percent

QUIZ 68

1. Four hundred
2. Astonishment
3. An amoeba
4. Captain Satak
5. Starbase 6 for R & R
6. By exploding an antimatter bomb at its nucleus
7. Bacteria
8. Enzyme recorder
9. Three
10. Kirk, Chekov, and Kyle

QUIZ 69

1. Five
2. A cold-steel drill point
3. Mugato
4. Nona
5. Dr. M'Benga
6. One hundred
7. Mako root
8. Apella
9. Tyree
10. A phaser

QUIZ 70

1. Astrobiologist
2. Arret
3. Eight
4. A half million years
5. Spock's
6. One thousand years
7. 104 degrees Fahrenheit
8. Sick Bay
9. Nurse Chapel
10. Metabolic reduction injections

QUIZ 71

1. Thermonuclear missile
2. John Gill
3. To give the transporter beam something to lock onto if communications are impossible
4. Daras; Iron Cross, second class
5. Isak's fiancée
6. Two transponders containing rubindium crystals and a light bulb
7. Melakon, using a machine gun
8. Colonel
9. Isak
10. Chairman Eneg

QUIZ 72

1. Tomar
2. She is reduced to a small block and crushed to powder
3. Three hundred years
4. Rigellian Kassaba fever
5. Formazine
6. Drea
7. Ganymede
8. Tomar
9. Immense beings with hundreds of tentacles
10. The Class-M planet where the *Enterprise* first found them

QUIZ 73

1. Engineering
2. Lt. Galloway
3. Holy Ay Pledgili
4. He beamed down to Omega IV where the atmosphere contained the necessary immunities
5. Fireboxes
6. Liyang
7. Four
8. Ten
9. "Freedom"
10. American and Chinese Communist

QUIZ 74

1. Z-Magnees and Nobel
2. Captain Harris
3. *Woden*
4. Fifty-three
5. Captain Dunsel
6. A-7 Computer Expert
7. Commodore Wesley
8. Murder
9. Finagle's Folly
10. "This unit must die"

QUIZ 75

1. S.S. *Beagle*
2. Planet 892-IV
3. Captain Merik
4. "Condition Green"
5. Ancient Roman
6. *Name the Winner*
7. Mars Toothpaste and Neptune Bath Salts
8. Achilles
9. A dagger
10. Christianity

QUIZ 76

1. McKinley Rocket Base
2. Supervisor 194
3. Highway 949
4. Cromwell
5. Somewhere over Asia
6. Roberta Lincoln
7. Colonel Nesvig
8. Police Sergeant Lipton
9. 811 East 68th Street, Apartment 12B, in New York
   City
10. Isis

QUIZ 77

1. Kara
2. Animation controller
3. The Controller
4. By following an ion trail
5. Three hours
6. Training device
7. Three
8. Transferral beam
9. Medical tricorder
10. Ten thousand years

QUIZ 78

1. Three
2. Tal
3. Two
4. Three weeks
5. Two months ago
6. Physiostimulator
7. Right of Statement
8. Cloaking device
9. Control Central
10. Tal

QUIZ 79

1. Honeysuckle
2. Navajo, Mohican, and Delaware
3. In hopes of destroying an asteroid on a collision course
4. Two stones
5. Salish
6. He revives a drowned boy
7. His father, who was to pass the secret on to him, died before the message could be transferred
8. Miramanee
9. The Preservers
10. By saying, "Kirk to Enterprise"

QUIZ 80

1. Cyalodin
2. Thirteen
3. Cocoanut and vanilla
4. Lacunar amnesia
5. In a cave
6. Mary Janowski
7. Marcos XII
8. Professor Wilkins
9. "Friendly Angel"
10. Starbase 4

QUIZ 81

1. Antarean brandy
2. A garment worn by the blind Dr. Jones which is covered with silver webbing, enabling her to know where she is, who is nearby, etc.
3. A visor
4. "I love you, Miranda."
5. Byron
6. Herbarium
7. Infinite Diversity in Infinite Combinations
8. *The Tempest*
9. 9.5
10. Dr. Miranda Jones

QUIZ 82

1. October 26, 1881
2. Five o'clock P.M.
3. Virgil Earp
4. Bourbon and corn whiskey
5. Sylvia
6. Johnny Behan
7. Morgan Earp
8. Taos lightning
9. Vulcan mind weld
10. To establish contact with the Melkots

QUIZ 83

1. Three years
2. Chekov
3. Mara
4. Sulu
5. "Fuzz-faced goon"
6. The hatred of others
7. Intra-ship beaming
8. Swords
9. Chekov
10. Forever

QUIZ 84

1. There is no known cure
2. Natira
3. A lonely life
4. Ten thousand years
5. Fabrina
6. The Instrument of Obedience
7. The eye
8. A weak tube
9. Xenopolycythemia
10. In the vast memory banks containing the knowledge of the Fabrini

QUIZ 85

1. U.S.S. *Defiant*
2. Three weeks
3. Lt. O'Neil
4. Two hours and twelve minutes
5. "Take care"
6. Commander Loskene
7. A Theragen derivative
8. Alcohol
9. Territorial annex of the Tholian Assembly
10. Never

QUIZ 86

1. Parmen
2. Alexander
3. Psychokinetic
4. A collection of herbs that once belonged to Hippocrates
5. Kironide
6. Lt. Uhura and Nurse Chapel
7. "I guess we weren't sufficiently entertaining"
8. His pituitary gland (that caused his dwarfness) also rejects the psychokinetic-causing kironide
9. "Maiden Wine"
10. Philana

QUIZ 87

1. From their appearance in their paintings
2. Compton
3. Hyperacceleration
4. A buzzing insect
5. Because of the hyperacceleration, the phaser's energy beam is emitted so slowly that it is easily dodged
6. Scott and Sulu
7. Volcano
8. Breeding
9. Rael
10. To repair the damage done to the *Enterprise* at the accelerated speed

QUIZ 88

1. Minara
2. McCoy
3. Sandbats
4. Psalms
5. An energy-transfer device transported them
6. Dr. Ozaba and Dr. Linke
7. Kirk
8. Brain damage
9. The race of mutes
10. McCoy's

QUIZ 89

1. Lord Petri
2. Her tears contain chemicals causing the behavior
3. As a peace gesture
4. Dilithium crystals
5. Colladium trioxide in a gobarium solution (Test 24)
6. Nuclear hand-guns
7. Elas
8. The bridegroom's mother
9. Radans
10. Starboard side of the *Enterprise*

QUIZ 90

1. Fifteen
2. Lord Garth
3. On Antos IV
4. "Queen to Queen's level three"
5. Ultrasonic
6. Heir apparent
7. One grain
8. A chair
9. "Queen to King's level one"
10. King Solomon

QUIZ 91

1. Starbase 4
2. Two weeks
3. Fifty thousand years
4. Left
5. To decontaminate the planet
6. Directional control and self-destruct banks
7. Twice
8. None
9. They activate their shields
10. They killed themselves

QUIZ 92

1. Vegan choriomeningitis
2. Admiral Fitzgerald
3. To curb the overpopulation
4. Blood was taken to use to infect Odona
5. Krodak
6. The crew
7. Not letting him accompany him to Gideon
8. Five
9. Daughter
10. Spock

QUIZ 93

1. Lt. D'Amato
2. Ensign Wyatt
3. Lt. Rhada
4. One thousand light years
5. By touching them, she causes "cellular disruption"
6. Nothing
7. Blocks her path
8. Warp 15.20
9. Scott
10. A defense computer

QUIZ 94

1. To transfer equipment to Memory Alpha
2. Martian Colony 3
3. Scotty
4. Jacques and Lydia
5. Standard Steinman analysis
6. Security Condition 3
7. Warp 2.6
8. Ten
9. Star Fleet Chief Engineer
10. Mira is placed in an atmospheric pressure chamber which causes extreme pressure differences from the vacuum the "lights" were accustomed to

QUIZ 95

1. Ryetalyn
2. Brahms
3. Galileo, Socrates, and Moses
4. Mr. Brack
5. "Field density and its relationship to gravity phenomenon"
6. Mesopotamia
7. Envy
8. Kirk
9. Bubonic plague
10. Love

QUIZ 96

1. Research engineer of acoustics
2. Space studies
3. Botany
4. An egg
5. Adam
6. *Aurora*
7. Spock
8. Mavig
9. Dr. Sevrin
10. Green with red stripes

QUIZ 97

1. Twenty percent
2. Federation Bureau of Industrialization
3. Five
4. Sentinels
5. Intentionally traps token Troglytes in a mine with the gas, then an hour later witnesses the obvious effect
6. To repair damaged entrance panels
7. Protectors
8. Rostrum
9. Mortae
10. To counteract the plague on Merak II

QUIZ 98

1. Carbon-cycle life forms
2. One thousand square kilometers
3. Lt. Dickerson
4. Four hours
5. General Ulysses S. Grant
6. Colonel Green
7. Excalbia
8. Zora
9. Negress
10. Kahless

QUIZ 99

1. Beta Niobe
2. Mr. Atoz
3. Atavachron
4. Zarabeth
5. Used for the preparation of someone who is permanently traveling to the past
6. Coradrenalin
7. Angler
8. Animal flesh
9. Zor Khan the Tyrant
10. Twenty thousand

QUIZ 100

1. U.S.S. *Potemkin*
2. One year
3. Celebium poisoning
4. McCoy's position
5. Mutiny
6. Starbase 2
7. Angela
8. Exploring ancient ruins
9. Incompetency
10. He loved her

The Best in Science Fiction from SIGNET Books